INSIDE MY BODY

STOMACH

WRITTEN BY ANNETTE BAY PIMENTEL ILLUSTRATED BY TERESA ALBERINI

amicus illustrated

Amicus Illustrated is published by Amicus
P.O. Box 1329, Mankato, MN 56002
www.amicuspublishing.us

Library of Congress Cataloging-in-Publication Data
Pimentel, Annette Bay, author.
 My stomach / by Annette Bay Pimentel ; Illustrated
by Teresa Alberini.
     pages cm. — (Inside my body) (Amicus illustrated)
 Summary: "Tim insists on telling his sister Grace all
about the digestive system while their father is sick
with a stomachache"—Provided by publisher.
 Audience: K to grade 3.
 ISBN 978-1-60753-758-8 (library binding) —
ISBN 978-1-60753-857-8 (ebook)
1. Stomach—Juvenile literature. 2. Digestion—
Juvenile literature. 3. Human physiology—Juvenile
literature. [1. Digestive system.] I. Alberini, Teresa,
illustrator. II. Title.
 QP151.P56 2016
 612.3'2—dc23   2014041493

Editor: Rebecca Glaser
Designer: Kathleen Petelinsek

Printed in the United States of America at
Corporate Graphics in North Mankato, Minnesota.

10 9 8 7 6 5 4 3 2 1

ABOUT THE AUTHOR

Annette Bay Pimentel writes magazine
stories and articles as well as books for
children. Four of her children are all grown
up, but two of them are still working on it.
She lives with them and her husband in
Bluffton, Ohio. Visit her on the web at
www.annettebaypimentel.com.

ABOUT THE ILLUSTRATOR

Teresa Alberini has always loved painting
and drawing. She attended the Academy
of Fine Arts in Florence, Italy, and she now
lives and works as an illustrator in a small
town on the Italian coast. Visit her on the
web at www.teresaalberini.com.

"Shhh! Dad's stomach hurts. He needs to rest."
"He probably ate too much. Do you know how your stomach works, Grace?"

"No. But I know I want a snack."

"Eating starts everything! Your body needs food. But the apple is too big for your body to use."

"My teeth turn it into mush before I swallow."

"Yes, they do! Your saliva helps that happen."

"Saliva?"

"It's a fancy word for spit. It softens your food."

"Oh. Well, I'm done. Let's go play outside."

"You may be done with your apple, Grace. But digestion just started!"

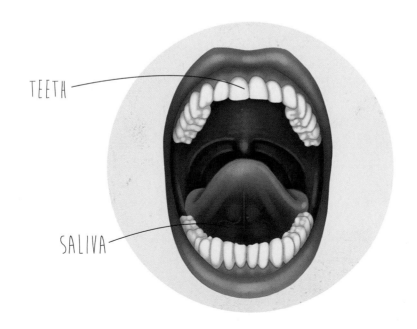

TEETH

SALIVA

"Your esophagus has already squeezed the apple pieces into your stomach, Grace."

"What's an ee-SOFF-uh-gus?"

"It's the tube from your mouth to your stomach."

"Oh! Kind of like the tube slide?"

"Kind of, but the tube slide doesn't squeeze you!"

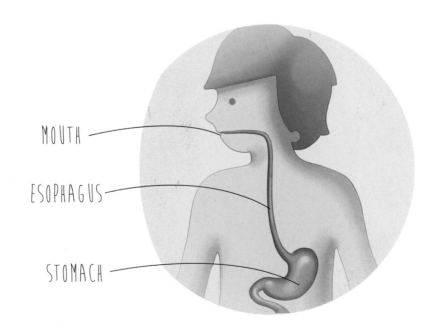

MOUTH

ESOPHAGUS

STOMACH

STOMACH

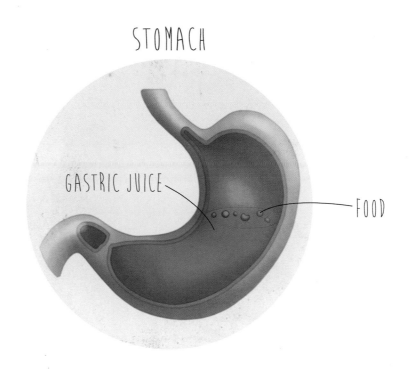

GASTRIC JUICE

FOOD

"So now my stomach mixes up the apple?"

"Yes. It mashes up your food. But if you eat too much at once, you get a stomachache like Dad."

"I see. Now my body can use the apple, right?"

"Not quite. You need gastric juice, too."

"What's gastric juice?"

"Liquid your stomach makes. It breaks down food into tinier bits. Everything ends up as a thick sludge."

"That sounds gross, Tim. But I'm hot. Let's fill the wading pool."

14

"This hose reminds me of something, Grace. Your food's journey isn't done yet."

"I should have known."

"Your food goes to the small intestine next. It's about as long as this hose. And it needs a little help."

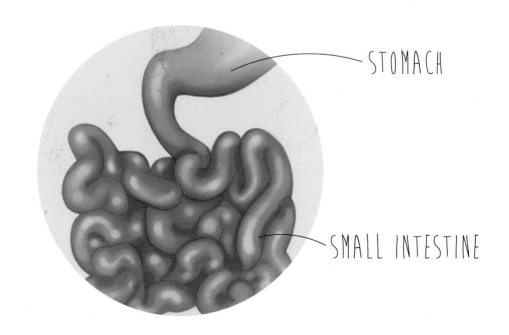

STOMACH

SMALL INTESTINE

"Help? What do you mean?"

"The liver, gall bladder, and pancreas all have tubes like the hose. They squirt chemicals onto the food."

"Why do they squirt chemicals, Tim? Not to cool off."

"Nope. They dissolve fats and nutrients. Finally the food bits are small enough."

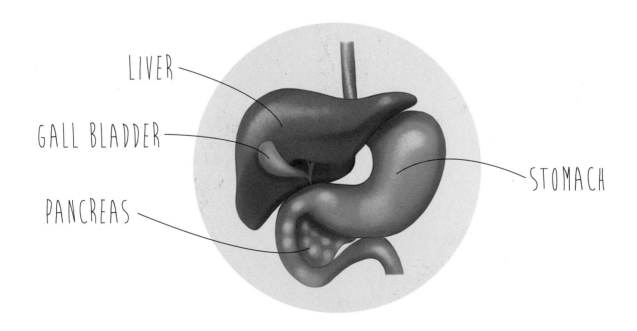

LIVER

GALL BLADDER

PANCREAS

STOMACH

"So is the small intestine the end?"

"Your blood picks up the nutrients from the small intestine and takes them around your body."

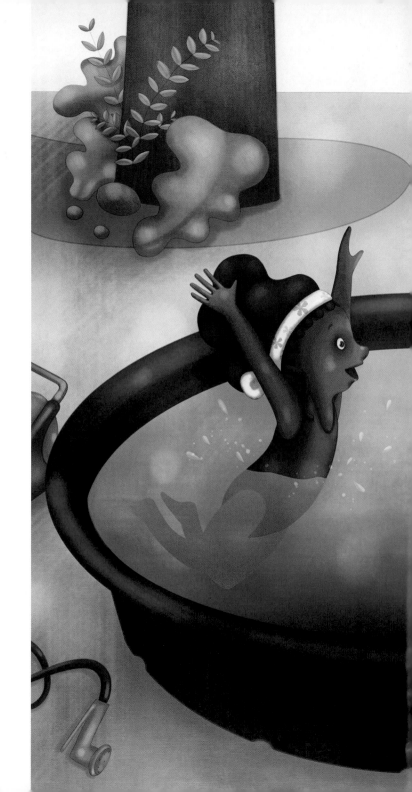

"So finally my body can use the energy from my apple?"

"Yes. And food lets you think and move and grow."

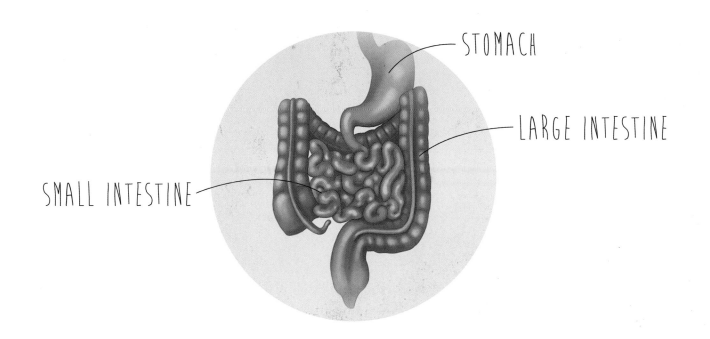

STOMACH

LARGE INTESTINE

SMALL INTESTINE

"Wow, Tim. Do you think we should check on Dad?"

"He's probably sleeping. And we're not done yet!"

"There's more?"

"Your body can't use some parts of food. They move into the large intestine."

"And then what?"

"Food scraps get made into poop."

"That must really be the end."

"Until the next time you eat!"

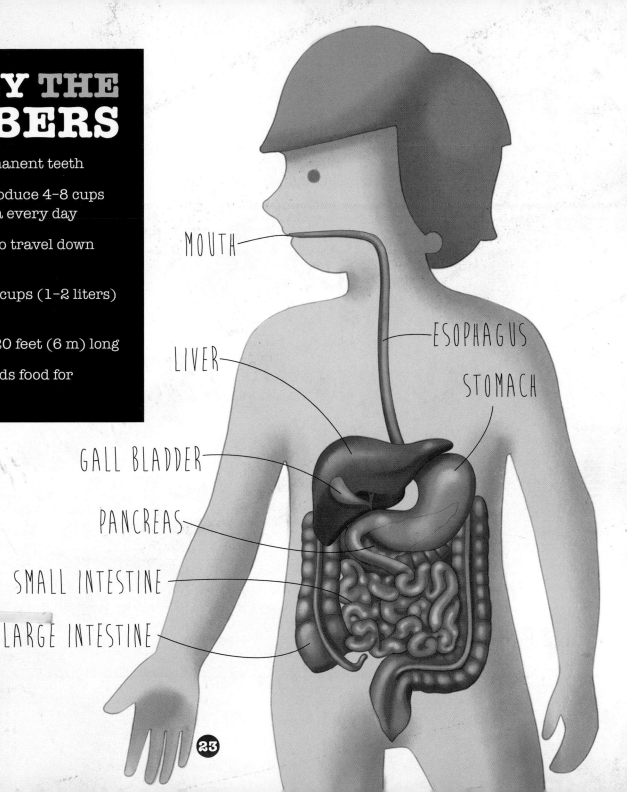

BODY BY THE NUMBERS

Mouth has 32 permanent teeth

Salivary glands produce 4–8 cups (1–2 liters) of saliva every day

5 seconds for food to travel down the esophagus

Stomach holds 4–8 cups (1–2 liters) of food

Small intestine is 20 feet (6 m) long

Large intestine holds food for 30–40 hours

MOUTH

ESOPHAGUS

LIVER

STOMACH

GALL BLADDER

PANCREAS

SMALL INTESTINE

LARGE INTESTINE

esophagus—The tube that connects the mouth to the stomach.

gastric juice—Liquid made by the stomach to help break food into tiny pieces.

large intestine—The large tube at the end of the digestive system where poop is made.

liver—A body part that makes chemicals to help break down nutrients.

saliva—A liquid made in your mouth that helps make food soft so you can swallow it.

small intestine—A long tube where nutrients from food enter the blood.

READ MORE

Han, Hyun-dong and Gomdori co. **Survive! Inside the Human Body, Volume 1: The Digestive System**. San Francisco: No Starch Press, 2013.

Johnson, Rebecca L. **Your Digestive System**. Minneapolis: Lerner, 2013.

Kolpin, Molly. **A Tour of Your Digestive System**. North Mankato, Minn.: Capstone, 2013.

WEBSITES

The Children's University of Manchester: The Digestive System
www.childrensuniversity.manchester.ac.uk/interactives/science/bodyandmedicine/digestivesystem/
Animated diagrams help explain how the stomach and digestive system work.

Interactive Human: Digestion Interactive Game for Kids
interactivehuman.blogspot.com/2008/05/digestion-interactive-game-for-kids.html
Up close details about what happens to your food as it goes through your body.

KidsHealth: How the Body Works
kidshealth.org/kid/htbw/
View movies, do activities, and read more about how all parts of your body work.

Every effort has been made to ensure that these websites are appropriate for children. However, because of the nature of the Internet, it is impossible to guarantee that these sites will remain active indefinitely or that their contents will not be altered.